COLLABORATIVE MATH BOOKS

For Your Class to Make and Share!

Easy Patterns for Creating
12 Adorable Rhyming Books That Build
Early Math & Literacy Skills

By Mary Beth Spann

My Wiggly Teeth
by Mr. Martin's
class

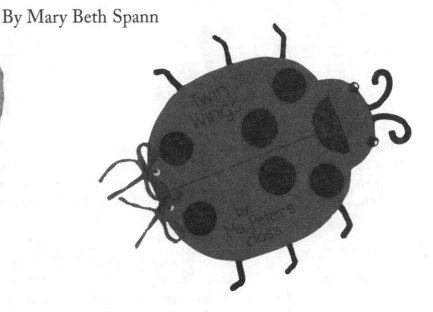

Twin Wings

by
Ms. Peter's
class

SCHOLASTIC
PROFESSIONAL BOOKS

New York • Toronto • London • Auckland • Sydney • Mexico City
New Delhi • Hong Kong

Dedication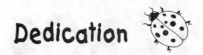

To Frank, Francesca, and James—
When I add up all the love and joy you've given me, the sum is infinity.

Acknowledgments

Heartfelt thanks to Scholastic editors Terry Cooper and Liza Charlesworth who never fail to support and inspire me. Thanks also to two talented women, Robin Bromley and Lauren Leon, for helping to edit and design this book to completion. And kudos to Theresa Fitzgerald who brought the collection of collaborative book covers to life with a warm and cheery touch, and to Jaime Lucero and Donnelly Marks for the beautifully designed and photographed cover on this book.

—MBS

Cover design by Jaime Lucero
Cover photography by Donnelly Marks
Cover and interior illustration by Rusty Fletcher
Sample books created by Theresa Fitzgerald
Interior design by LDL Designs

ISBN 0-590-64192-1

Table of Contents

Introduction
Welcome to the world of collaborative books!

With this easy and fun-filled approach to bookmaking, each student author completes one reproducible book page. The completed pages are then bound together in a polished publication for children to enjoy in class and to take home and share with their families.

Our first collection of reproducible collaborative books—*30 Collaborative Books for Your Class to Make and Share!*—invited children to create a year's worth of thematic books. In this new collection, we've designed math collaboratives to help make your math program sparkle. Basic math skills and concepts in each rhyming selection ensure students many chances to write and read about math, and to use math to learn about the world around them.

Children love creating this library of original books. And each time they complete one, they revel in their ability to read and write with growing ease and proficiency. Even family members appreciate sharing and responding to the books. So read on to learn how your class can begin publishing its own math books today!

What Collaborative Books Add to the Classroom

• Collaborative books foster cooperation while showcasing each child's unique contribution.

• They are easy-to-facilitate writing projects. Because all of the children are working on the same selection, you stay focused while helping each writer complete his or her own page.

• The approach fosters respect for others' work. Each child sees the different ways his or her classmates respond to the same selection.

• Because all of the selections in this book are zippy, easy-to-learn rhymes, children gain confidence reading the selections to themselves and to their friends and families.

• The small, shape-book format delights children and is easy to tote home. Just slip the book into a self-closing plastic bag and it's ready to go!

• Families love reading collaborative books. Each book gives them a window into the classroom—allowing them to see how their children and their classmates are progressing in writing. Plus, the books offer families a terrific opportunity to respond (see Family Feedback, page 7).

How to Use This Book

This book contains 12 rhyming selections in six different shape books (two selections per shape). The rhymes and shapes have been designed to enhance common early elementary math skills and concepts.

To help move the bookmaking process along smoothly from prewriting to publication, each selection is presented with the following teaching guidelines:

1. Prewriting Warm-up

This sets the stage for the writing to come. Simple discussion ideas help children cross the bridge from what they know to what they will write about.

2. Introducing the Selection

Here you'll find specific ideas for reading and reciting each selection. Because every selection offers children a blank space to fill in or an open-ended question to answer, each one provides an easy-to-use framework for children's early writing attempts and practice the math skills they are learning.

Before introducing each selection, print the poem on sentence strips (for use with a pocket chart), chart pad paper, or the chalkboard. Then you can introduce it to the whole group at once. **Tip:** When presenting a selection to the whole group, always fill the blanks with possible responses. Initially, blank spaces can be confusing to children trying to read, so when preparing a selection, draw lines indicating blank spaces, and then use sticky notes [with chart paper] or sentence-strip cards [with a pocket chart] to print possible responses in the blanks.

3. Writing Together

This section helps you learn how to make the most of students' writing efforts. Because many of the selections ask children to respond by counting and recording a number, you can expand the writing opportunities by having them draw and label a corresponding illustration, or by having them write a sentence explaining their math reasoning. To help with this, provide children with sticky notes on which they can jot a rough draft of their response using developmental spelling. (Unlike scrap paper, sticky notes tend to stay put and don't get lost in the shuffle.)

Next, meet briefly with students individually to help them check and polish their efforts. Explain that because their collaborative books will be published for other people's eyes, their work must be edited and polished so it is easy to read and best conveys what they mean to say. As part of the editing process, have them recopy (or you may need to recopy for them) their revisions on a second sticky note before they transfer the final version to the shape page. Because the expected writing is minimal, even children with the most limited writing experience can complete this editing step successfully.

4. Illustrating Pages

Encourage children to finish their pages by drawing and labeling an illustration that tells about the selection they have completed. Adding an illustration gives children a chance to personalize the page, so the invitation to illustrate should be kept as open-ended as possible. **Tip:** Remind children not to color over the words printed on the page.

5. Back-Cover Bonus

Look here for suggested math questions, brain teasers, and puzzlers for you to write on the inside the back cover of the book. The bonus ideas always relate to the math skills and concepts presented in the collaborative book.

6. Extension Activity

Here you'll find hints, follow-up activities, and suggestions for keeping the learning alive long after the book has been completed.

7. Best-Book Connection

Look here for recommended children's books hand picked to enhance each selection's themes and math concepts. These titles enrich and support the bookmaking process.

The Steps to Publishing a Collaborative Book

When making any of the collaborative math books, refer to the teaching guidelines that accompany each selection. Then follow these simple steps:

1. Choose a shape-book cover and rhyme.

2. Copy at least one page per child, so everyone can contribute to the book.

3. Present the topic and selection to the class.

4. Have children respond to the math problem then write and illustrate their page.

5. Bind completed pages between the matching book covers prepared from the reproducible templates.

6. Read and share your finished publication. Then send it home for families to enjoy.

Additional Publishing Tips

These production tips will help polish your book presentation:

• Photocopy the book cover pattern directly onto construction paper. Make four copies, so you can glue together two for the front and two for the back cover or you may choose to cut covers from oak tag after tracing the shape of the cover.

• Ask for volunteers to decorate the covers using crayons, paint, or markers.

• Laminate the covers or protect them with a clear self-adhesive paper.

• For truly captivating covers, look for the Cover Design ideas on the first page of each new book.

• If possible, copy the pages directly onto drawing paper cut to fit your copy machine. Drawing paper more readily accepts the crayon, paint, or colored markers that children will use for their illustrations.

• Copy and cut additional shape pages to serve a follows:

   — a title page,

   — a dedication page (complete with copyright information and the name of your class publishing house),

   — Family Feedback pages (to be placed in the back of the book) inviting family members to offer their comments,

   — an About the Authors and Illustrators page that includes a class photo (copied on the copy machine) along with a short write-up about the children and their interests.

• Use a paper punch to punch holes in each page and in the covers, as indicated on the templates. (An electric hole punch really cuts this job down to size.) Reinforce each hole with a self-sticking loose-leaf hole reinforcer. After arranging pages in order, bind them by threading loose-leaf rings, ribbons, yarn, or pipe cleaners (twisted together to form rings) through the holes. Number the pages, if desired.

Family Feedback

Your children had a delicious time preparing this pizza-shaped book that taught about fractions. We want to know what you think of our book. Please add comments below. Thank you.

3/30 Our compliments to the chefs! You really cooked up a fun-to-read book. We can't wait to sample your class's next book
—The Hernandez Family

4/5 This was the best pizza we ever read!
—The Sullivans

About the Authors and Illustrators

Ms. Smith's first grade enjoyed making this collaborative math book about how much pizza they eat. They were pleased to learn the fractional equivalents of their pizza meals. This book made them so hungry, they decided to make some real pizzas in class. They are currently figuring out how many pizzas they will need to prepare so each student can enjoy a piece. Yummy!

Suggestions for Sharing the Books

When your book is bound, the fun's just begun! Here are some special ways to get the most mileage out of your publications:

• When each child completes a page, ask him or her to share it with the class. Also ask children to explain how they arrived at their responses, showing that there are a variety of ways to figure out a problem.

• Keep the books in your class library, so children can read them as they do other books you make available. Of course, it's always wise to hold a discussion from time to time about the importance of caring for books, but children usually are careful with their own publications. If the books begin to show wear, simply add a bit more reinforcement or a fresh book cover. **Tip:** This refurbishing process is a good job for parents who wish to help from home.

• Before the first book goes home, provide parents with a take-home letter describing the program and its benefits (see sample, opposite page). Also, remember to check the "Family Feedback" pages from time to time. Comments from parents and other family members can offer you a real boost and can give you ideas for future books.

• Tuck the books in self-closing plastic bags when sending them home with students.

• Hold a book fair and invite parents and other classes to view your collection.

• One great feature of the collaborative book pages is that they feature self-contained rhymes. At year's end you can disassemble each book and bind each student's pages together to form individual collections for everyone to keep and treasure.

No matter what kind of writing program you have in place, these books will be a welcome addition to your curriculum. And you surely will be pleased in the writing that results. Let us know how the program turns out for you. We'd love to hear your success stories.

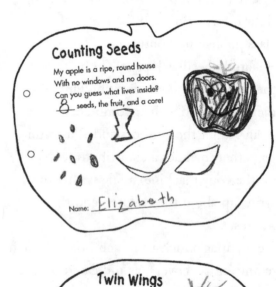

Sample Letter to Families

Dear Families:

This year our class will be publishing a series of collaborative math books. The books are designed to help children integrate math skills and concepts with writing.

For each book project, all of the children will complete the same open-ended rhyme printed on a shape page. The children will personalize the pages by adding their own responses and illustrations. I will help the children to edit their responses for publication (so everyone reading their page will understand what they are trying to say). These finished pages will then be bound together in a book and circulated among your homes for you to enjoy together. There's even a Family Feedback page, so you can share your comments with the class.

When sharing these books at home, your child may want to read the rhyming verse printed on every page. That's great! It's one sign that your child is beginning to feel comfortable, confident, and competent with print. Other benefits of making and sharing these books include:

- fostering math skills and concepts,
- fostering reading skills,
- fostering writing and editing skills,
- learning to respect one another's work, and
- generating self-esteem.

We're very excited about our math book program. If you'd like to help out, either from home or in class, please contact me.

Thank you for your support!

Sincerely,

Your child's teacher

Sharing Apples
by Ms. Sorvillo's Class

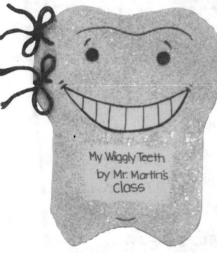

My Wiggly Teeth
by Mr. Martin's
class

The 12 Collaborative Math Books

Twin Wings
by Ms. Peter's
class

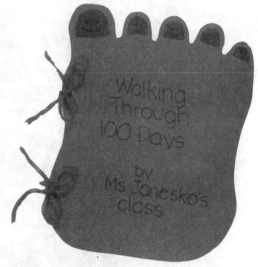

Walking Through 100 Days
by Ms. Janesko's
class

Pizza Pieces by Mr. Mephan's class

Thumbs Up!
by Mr. Lucero's
Class

Fancy Foot

Kick off the first day of school with these two foot-book selections. The first asks children to count the toes in their family. The second asks them to count and celebrate the first 100 days of school.

Walking Through 100 Days

by Ms. Janesko's class

COVER DESIGN IDEA

Cut out book covers from a fanciful shade of oak tag, such as fluorescent green or blue. Paint toenails with real nail polish—perhaps in a rainbow of colors! Or add five friendly little faces.

Fancy Foot Cover Template

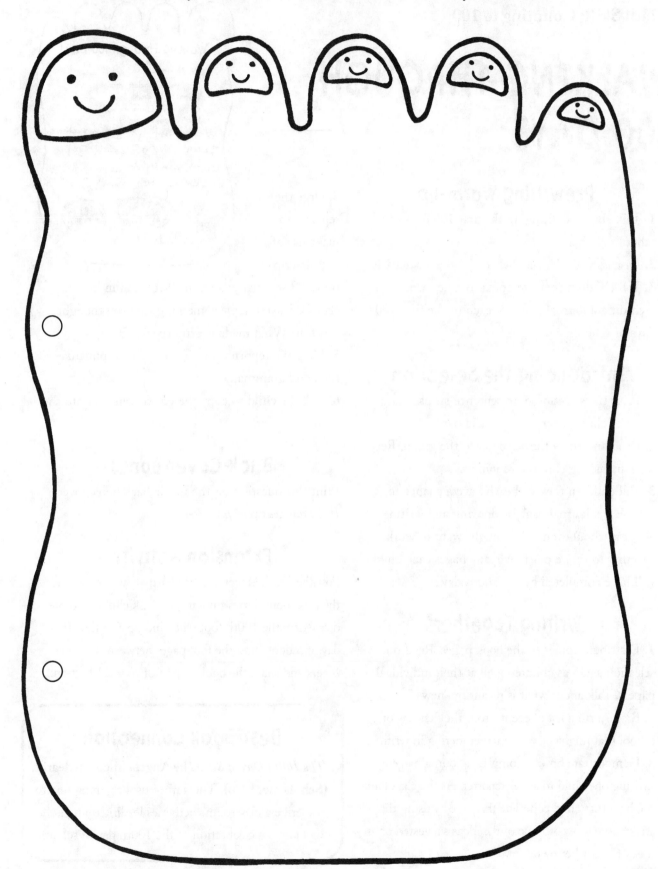

Fancy Foot Selection A
Math Skill: Counting to 100

WALKING THROUGH 100 DAYS

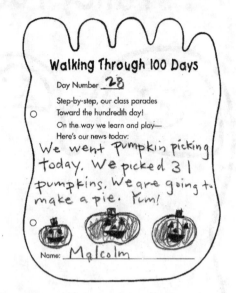

Walking Through 100 Days

Day Number **28**

Step-by-step, our class parades
Toward the hundredth day!
On the way we learn and play—
Here's our news today:

We went pumpkin picking today. We picked 31 pumpkins. We are going to make a pie. Yum!

Name: **Malcolm**

Prewriting Warm-up

1. Talk about counting up the first 100 days of school together.

2. Discuss with the class what a journal or diary is.

3. Tell children they are going to take turns recording a journal page for each of the first 100 days of school.

Introducing the Selection

1. Print the selection onto sentence strips, a large sheet of chart paper, or the chalkboard.

2. Read and show the selection to the group. Read it again, asking children to join in.

3. Tell children they will each have a chance to complete a journal page by drawing and writing about a school event. (You might want to work together to figure out how many pages each child will have completed by the 100th day.)

Writing Together

1. Distribute copies of the book pages. Read the selection again as children look at their individual papers. Talk about what is meant by "news."

2. Brainstorm a list of events from the first day of school that might be worth remembering in writing.

3. Demonstrate how to complete a journal page by inviting one child to act as reporter. As the class looks on, help that child complete the page by using the sticky note to record one of the ideas suggested or an idea of his or her own.

4. Urge the reporter to make use of rich descriptions. ("I see that you wrote, 'We had fun in gym class.' Can you name something that you thought was fun? What made it extra special?")

5. Help the reporter polish the spelling, punctuation, and grammar.

6. Ask the child to copy the edited version onto the shape page and to add an illustration.

Back-Cover Bonus

Print this question on the inside back book cover: *What day was your favorite?*

Extension Activity

Post the finished feet in a border that "walks" around the classroom. From time to time, ask children to predict where the 100th foot will wind up. On the 100th day of school, bind the foot pages between the book covers and share the book as part of your celebration.

Best-Book Connection

The 100th Day of School **by Angela Shelf Medearis (Scholastic, 1996).** The author uses rhyming text to describe a classroom's activities leading up to, and including, a celebration of the 100th day of school.

Fancy Foot Selection A Template

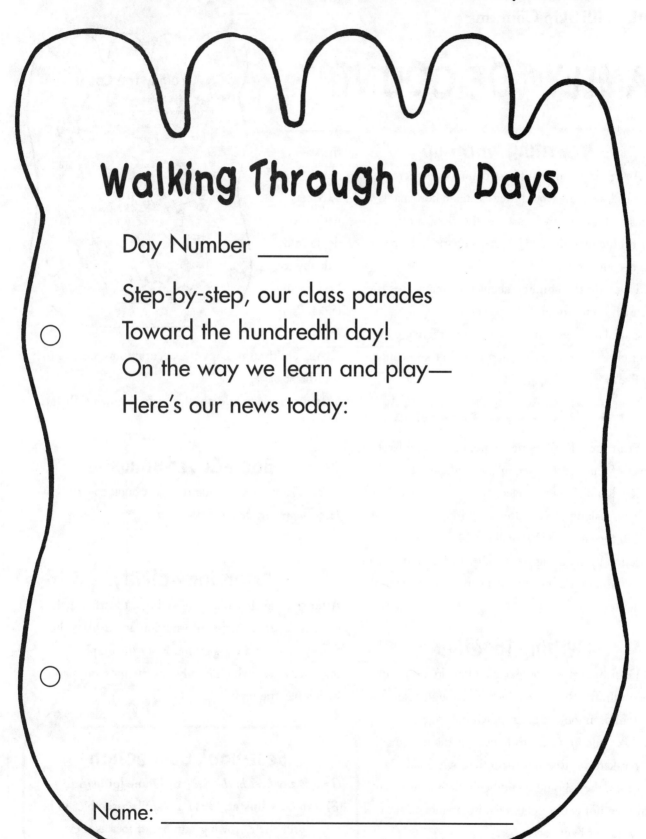

Walking Through 100 Days

Day Number _____

Step-by-step, our class parades
Toward the hundredth day!
On the way we learn and play—
Here's our news today:

Name: _____

FAMILY TOE COUNT

Family Toe Count

Tickle, tickle, tickle toes—
five are on each foot, you know!
So count by fives and you will see
the sum of toes in your family!

In my family there are ___30___ toes in all.

Name: _Carmen_

Prewriting Warm-up

1. Ask children to count how many noses there are in the class. How would they calculate how many arms and how many legs are in the class? **Tip:** Distribute reproducible hundreds charts to help students count by two's.

2. Talk with the children about how many toes they have on each foot and altogether.

3. Calculate how many feet and toes there are in your class. **Tip:** Use the chart to help them count by five's.

Introducing the Selection

1. Print the selection onto sentence strips, a large sheet of chart pad paper, or the chalkboard.

2. Read and show the selection to the group. Read it again, asking the children to chime in.

3. Tell the children they will be completing the selection by counting the number of feet and toes in their families (defined as the people they live with at home).

Writing Together

1. Distribute the book pages and sticky notes for rough drafts. Read the selection through again as the children look at their individual pages.

2. Ask children to try to figure out the information asked for. Remind them that, when calculating toes, they should count by five's. Suggest that children not count pets as family members, since they do not have toes.

3. Encourage children to record their answers on the sticky notes.

4. Meet with students individually to help them check their math.

5. Ask children to copy the accurate numbers onto the shape page.

6. Invite them to add an illustration showing their family's feet and toes.

Back-Cover Bonus

Print this question inside the back book cover:
How many big toes are in each family?

Extension Activity

After sharing the collaborative book together, help each child transfer the information about his or her family's toes to a class graph. Read the graph together to see which family has the most toes and which has the least.

Best-Book Connection

How Many Feet in the Bed? by Diane Johnston **(Simon & Schuster, 1991).** A family assembles in bed and counts their growing number of toes as they go.

Fancy Foot Selection B Template

Family Toe Count

Tickle, tickle, tickle toes—
five are on each foot, you know!
So count by fives and you will see
the sum of toes in my family!

In my family there are _____ toes in all.

Name: _____

Shiny Apple

What's more inviting than a sweet, shiny apple? How about an apple-shaped book just ripe for children to pick, write in, and read! The first Shiny Apple selection has children counting apple seeds. The second asks them to count and take away slices of apple before sharing an apple snack. Anyway you slice it, it's delicious core learning!

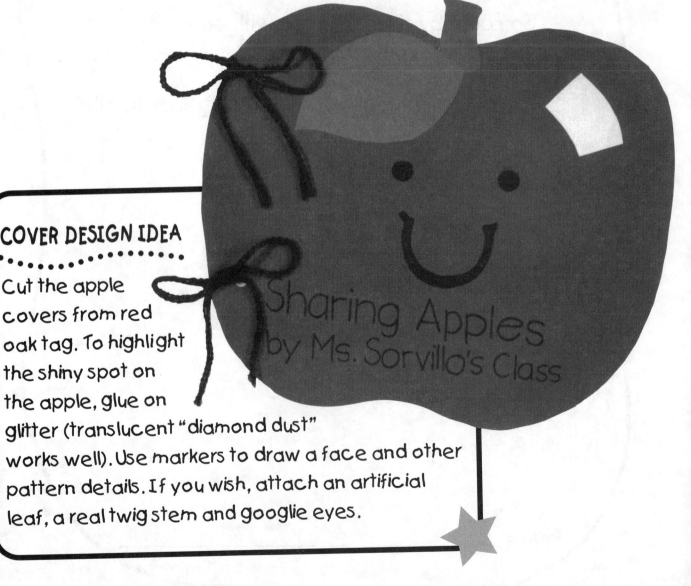

COVER DESIGN IDEA

Cut the apple covers from red oak tag. To highlight the shiny spot on the apple, glue on glitter (translucent "diamond dust" works well). Use markers to draw a face and other pattern details. If you wish, attach an artificial leaf, a real twig stem and googlie eyes.

Sharing Apples by Ms. Sorvillo's Class

Shiny Apple Cover Template

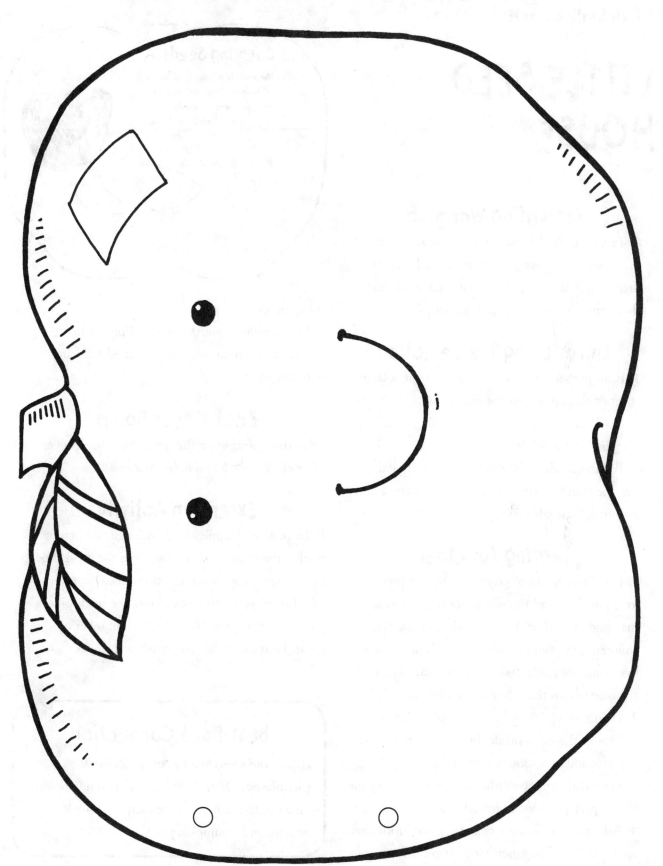

LITTLE SEED HOUSE

Counting Seeds

My apple is a ripe, round house
With no windows and no doors.
Can you guess what lives inside?
8 seeds, the fruit, and a core!

Name: Elizabeth

Prewriting Warm-up

1. Talk with children about where apples grow.

2. Explain that trees grow from seeds. Invite children to talk about planting seeds and watching them grow. What other fruit has seeds?

Introducing the Selection

1. Print the selection onto sentence strips, a large sheet of chart paper, or the chalkboard.

2. Read and show the selection to the group. Read it again, asking children to join in.

3. Tell the children they will each be completing the selection by first cutting open a real apple and counting the seeds inside.

Writing Together

1. Distribute the book pages and sticky notes for rough drafts. Read the selection through again as the children look at their individual pages. Tell children they might think of an apple as a protective house for seeds. Ask children if they know of any other foods that serve as seed houses.

2. Help each child cut open an apple and remove and count the seeds inside. Invite them to sample the fruit and look closely at the core.

3. Have children record the number of seeds in the blank space provided in the selection.

4. Ask them to illustrate what they saw inside their apples and to write labels for their pictures on the

sticky notes.

5. Help children polish their spelling, punctuation, and grammar, and copy their edited labels onto the page.

Back-Cover Bonus

Print this question on the inside back book cover:
How many seeds did your class find in all?

Extension Activity

Fill a bowl with apples and challenge children to predict the total number of seeds in the bowl. Then cut the apples open and count the seeds in each one. Graph your results by gluing the seeds onto a piece of graph paper. Add the total number of seeds. How close did the predictions come?

Best-Book Connection

Apples and Pumpkins by Anne Rockwell (Scholastic, 1989). This book takes young readers on a trip to the farm where there is an apple orchard and a pumpkin patch.

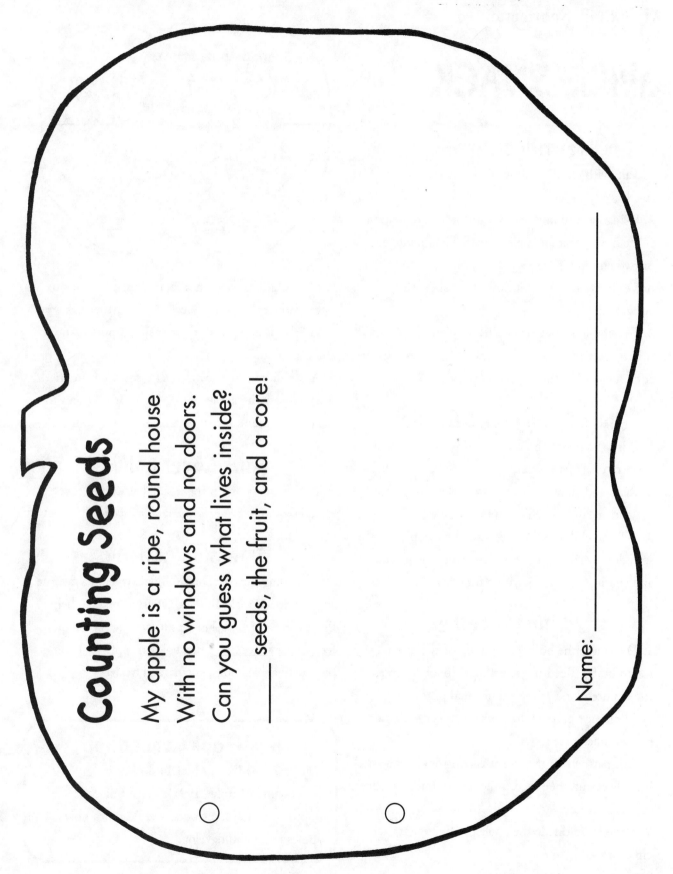

Counting Seeds

My apple is a ripe, round house

With no windows and no doors.

Can you guess what lives inside?

___ seeds, the fruit, and a core!

Name: _____

APPLE SNACK

Sharing Apple Snacks

We cut an apple for a snack—
4 pieces, crisp and sweet!
I gave my partner 2 of them.
That leaves 2 for me to eat!

Name: Sarah

Prewriting Warm-up

1. Talk with children about their favorite apple snacks.

2. Using a sharp knife and a cutting board, demonstrate how to cut an apple in half. Then invite one or two children to use a plastic knife to cut the halves into slices. Count how many slices they cut altogether.

3. Tell children they will each complete the selection by cutting an apple, counting the slices they cut, and sharing their apple with a friend.

Introducing the Selection

1. Print the selection onto sentence strips, a large sheet of chart pad paper, or the chalkboard.

2. Read and show the selection to the group. Read it again, asking the children to chime in.

3. Tell the children they will each be completing the selection by slicing an apple, counting the pieces, and sharing the pieces with a friend.

Writing Together

1. Distribute the book pages and sticky notes for rough drafts. Read the selection through again as the children look at their individual pages. Help children pick partners to work with. For each pair, pre-cut one apple in half.

2. Ask partners to take turns cutting apple halves into slices and then record the total number of slices on a sticky note.

3. Have them divide the apple pieces so that each child has some to eat.

4. Help children write numbers on sticky notes to reflect how many apple pieces each partner has.

5. Help children polish their spelling, punctuation, and grammar.

6. Ask children to draw a picture showing the math story of how the apple was divided. Invite them to use developmental spelling to label their pictures.

Back-Cover Bonus

Print this question on the inside back book cover: *How many apples did our class cut altogether?*

Extension Activity

After sharing the collaborative book, vote on a favorite apple recipe to make in class. Or ask parents to help the class work in small groups to prepare several different recipes at once. Then hold an apple feast complete with apple books, poems, and treats!

Best-Book Connection

Apples: Foods We Eat **by Rhode Nottridge (Carolrhoda Books, 1991).** With full-color photos, this book introduces children to how apples grow and develop.

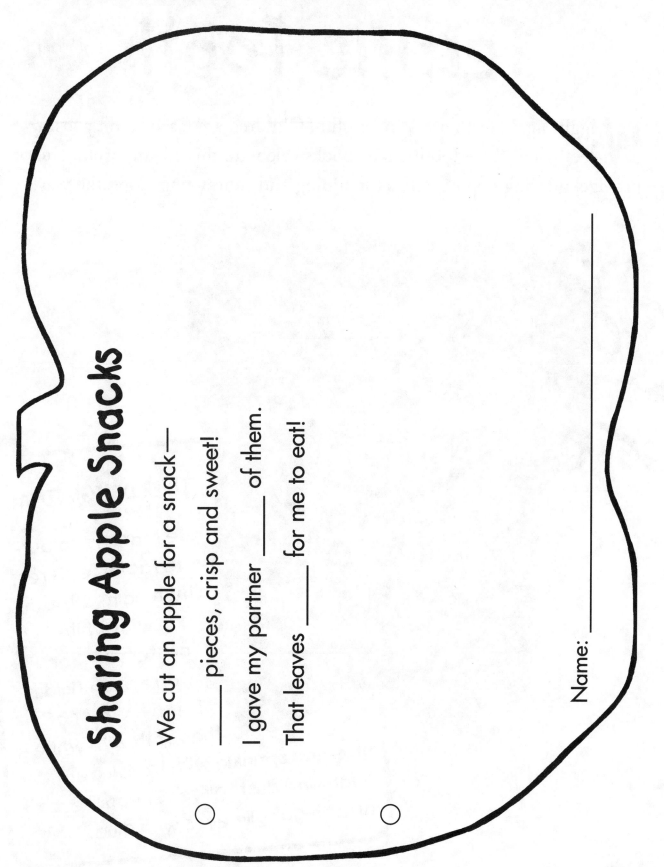

Sharing Apple Snacks

We cut an apple for a snack—
____ pieces, crisp and sweet!

I gave my partner ____ of them.

That leaves ____ for me to eat!

Name: _____

Terrific Tooth

Wiggly, jiggly teeth are so much fun. Children are fascinated by losing teeth, and these tooth-shape books celebrate this all-important rite of passage, offering opportunities for adding and subtracting along the way!

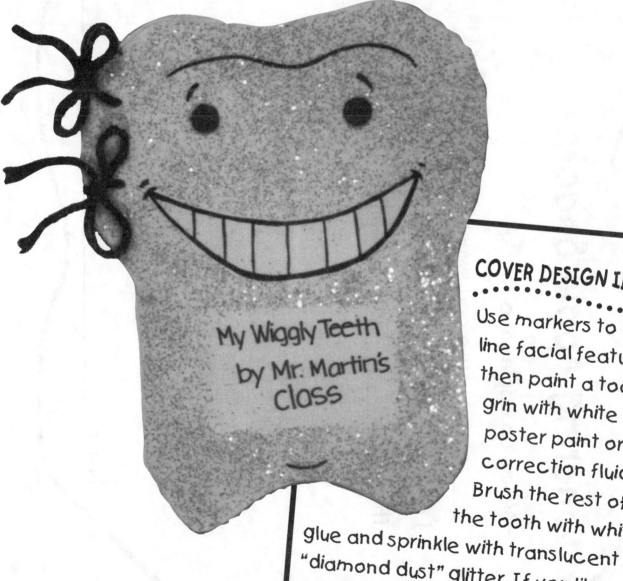

My Wiggly Teeth
by Mr. Martin's class

COVER DESIGN IDEA

Use markers to outline facial features, then paint a tooth grin with white poster paint or correction fluid. Brush the rest of the tooth with white glue and sprinkle with translucent "diamond dust" glitter. If you like, attach googlie eyes with glue.

Terrific Tooth Cover Template

COUNTING TEETH

Counting Teeth

I have lots of teeth on top
And plenty more on the bottom.
I brush and floss and then I smile—
'Cause I'm so glad I've got 'em!

I have this many top teeth: 8
I have this many bottom teeth: 10
I have this many teeth altogether: 18
This many teeth show when I smile: 7

Name: Stephen

Prewriting Warm-up

1. Find out what children already know about teeth. (For example, do they know what teeth do, how to care for them, and why baby teeth fall out?)

2. Ask children to recount trips to the dentist.

3. Tell children that they are going to make a tooth book that will have them each counting their teeth.

Introducing the Selection

1. Print the selection onto sentence strips, chart paper, or the chalkboard.

2. Read and show the selection to the group. Read it again, asking children to join in.

3. Tell children they will each be completing the selection by counting their own teeth and filling in the blank spaces with the correct numbers.

Writing Together

1. Distribute the book pages and sticky notes for rough drafts. Read the selection through again as the children look at their individual papers.

2. Put children in pairs and have them use a mirror to count their teeth. Have children check their partners' number counts by peeking into (not touching) one another's mouths.

3. Ask children to record the correct numbers on the sticky notes.

4. Meet with students individually to check their count and give them a chance to explain how they calculated their responses.

5. Invite them to add an illustration of their own smiling face.

Back-Cover Bonus

Print this question on the inside back book cover:
How many teeth has our whole class lost altogether?

Extension Activity

After sharing the collaborative book together, ask children to comment on the numbers generated. Ask: Why do some children have more teeth than others? Why have some children lost their teeth and others have not? Conclude by explaining that children grow and lose teeth at different rates, but that most children have 20 teeth and most adults have 32.

Best-Book Connection

Going to the Dentist: A Mr. Rogers' First Experience Book **by Fred Rogers and Jim Judkis (Putnam, 1989).** This book takes young readers on a realistic trip to the dentist's office. It teaches about tooth care, too.

Counting Teeth

I have lots of teeth on top
And plenty more on the bottom.
I brush and floss and then I smile—
'Cause I'm so glad I've got 'em!

I have this many top teeth: _____
I have this many bottom teeth: _____
I have this many teeth altogether: _____
This many teeth show when I smile: _____

Name: _____

Terrific Tooth Selection B
Math Skills: Counting, Subtraction

MY WIGGLY TEETH

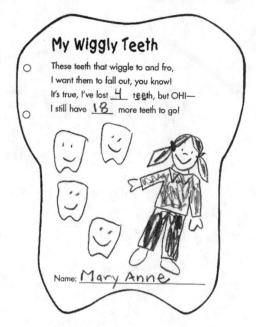

My Wiggly Teeth

These teeth that wiggle to and fro,
I want them to fall out, you know!
It's true, I've lost __4__ teeth, but OHI—
I still have __18__ more teeth to go!

Name: _Mary Anne_

Prewriting Warm-up

1. Ask children to tell what it feels like to have a wiggly tooth.

2. Reassure children that while some children's teeth do not fall out as fast as others, eventually everyone's baby teeth do fall out and are replaced by adult teeth.

Introducing the Selection

1. Print the selection on sentence strips, chart paper, or the chalkboard.

2. Read and show the selection to the group. Read it again, asking children to join in.

3. Tell children they will each be completing the selection by counting and recording the number of teeth they have lost and the number they have left to lose.

Writing Together

1. Distribute the book pages and sticky notes. Read the selection through again as the children look at their individual pages. Draw attention to the fact that blanks have been provided so children may turn t_ _th into *tooth* (singular) or *teeth* (plural).

2. Encourage children to use a mirror to count the number of teeth they have lost and how many they have left to go. Ask them to record their answers on the page.

3. Meet with students individually and encourage each to use sticky notes to record a sentence or two telling about a loose-tooth adventure. (They could tell about the first tooth they lost, for example, or about what the Tooth Fairy left as a gift).

4. Help students polish their spelling, punctuation, and grammar.

5. Ask children to copy the edited version onto the shape page.

6. Invite them to draw a scene from their loose-tooth adventure.

Back-Cover Bonus

Print this question on the inside back book cover:
Which child has the least number of teeth to lose?

Extension Activity

Invite a dental hygienist to come to class and show the children how to take care of their teeth.

Best-Book Connection

Arthur's Tooth by Marc Brown (Joy Street, 1987). Arthur is frustrated because he's the only one in his class who hasn't lost a tooth yet and he feels as though he never will.

Terrific Tooth Selection B Template

My Wiggly Teeth

These teeth that wiggle to and fro,
I want them to fall out, you know!
It's true, I've lost _____ t_ _th, but OH!—
I still have _____ more teeth to go!

Name: _____

Little Ladybug

Here's a little critter children really can count on! The first selection invites children to count ladybug spots and notice symmetry. The second asks them to notice ladybug colors.

Twin Wings

by Ms. Peter's class

COVER DESIGN IDEA

Cut out three cover shapes from red oak tag. On the front cover, attach black felt dots to the bug's wings and pipe-cleaner antennae to the head. Place black pipe cleaner legs between the remaining back book covers and glue together.

Little Ladybug Cover Template

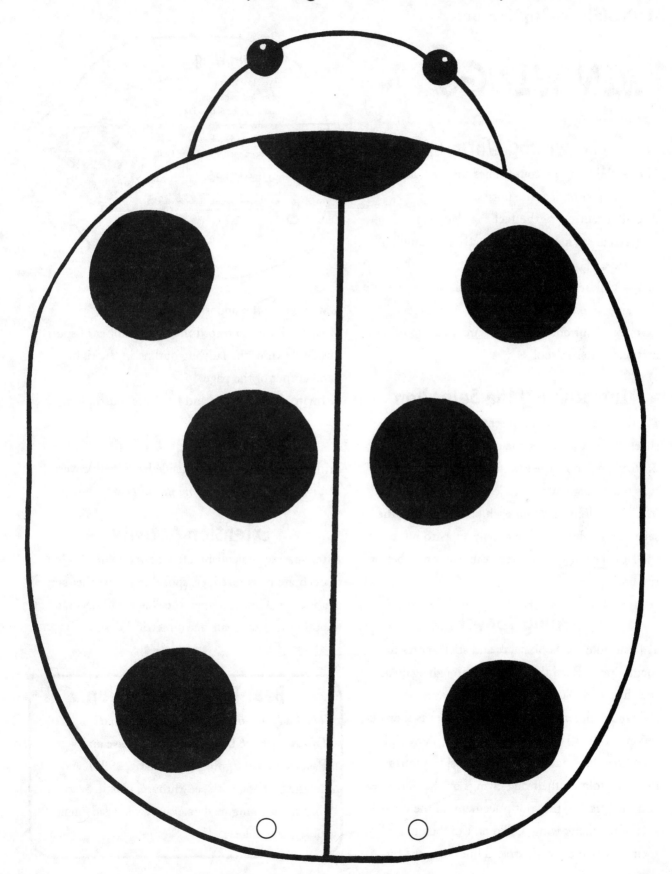

TWIN WINGS

Twin Wings

If you look at one
of my ladybug's wings
and count the dots so fine,
it's easy to know
the dots on the whole—
just double the number you find!

Name: _Carlos_

Cover one of my ladybug's wings. Guess how
many dots are on the whole bug. Turn the paper
upside-down to see if you are right.

My ladybug has _12_ spots in all.

Prewriting Warm-up

1. Ask children to recount times they saw ladybugs. Ask: Did you notice the spots?

2. Call attention to the fact that ladybug spot patterns are symmetrical—exactly the same on each side.

3. Ask children to find parts of their bodies that are the same on each side—ears, eyes, and fingers, for example. Point out that people are made up of symmetrical patterns, too.

Introducing the Selection

1. Print the selection onto sentence strips, a large sheet of chart paper, or the chalkboard.

2. Read and show the selection to the group. Read it again, asking children to join in.

3. Tell children they will each be completing the selection by deciding how many spots to put on the ladybug's wings and recording that number on the page.

Writing Together

1. Distribute the book pages and sticky notes for rough drafts. Read the selection through again as the children look at their individual pages.

2. Invite children to draw as many spots as they like on one of their ladybug's wings. Then, show children how they may make the other side a mirror image by folding their bug's wings on the mid-lines and then tracing the spot placement on the underside of the blank wing. Children can then unfold their papers and use the traced lines to make the

new spots on the opposite wing.

3. Ask children to record the total number of spots upside down in the ladybug outline in the right-hand corner of the page.

4. Invite them to color and label the illustration.

Back-Cover Bonus

Print this question on the inside back book cover:
How many ladybug wings are in this book?

Extension Activity

After sharing the collaborative book, invite children to decorate it with stripes, spots, or some other simple pattern. They can open the shape and decorate the other half to create a symmetrical design.

Best-Book Connection

The Ladybug and Other Insects : A First Discovery Book **by Galimard Jeunesse and Pascale de Bourgoing (Scholastic, 1991).** A delightful book with see-through plastic overlays that show young readers exactly what ladybugs look like up close.

Little Ladybug Selection A Template

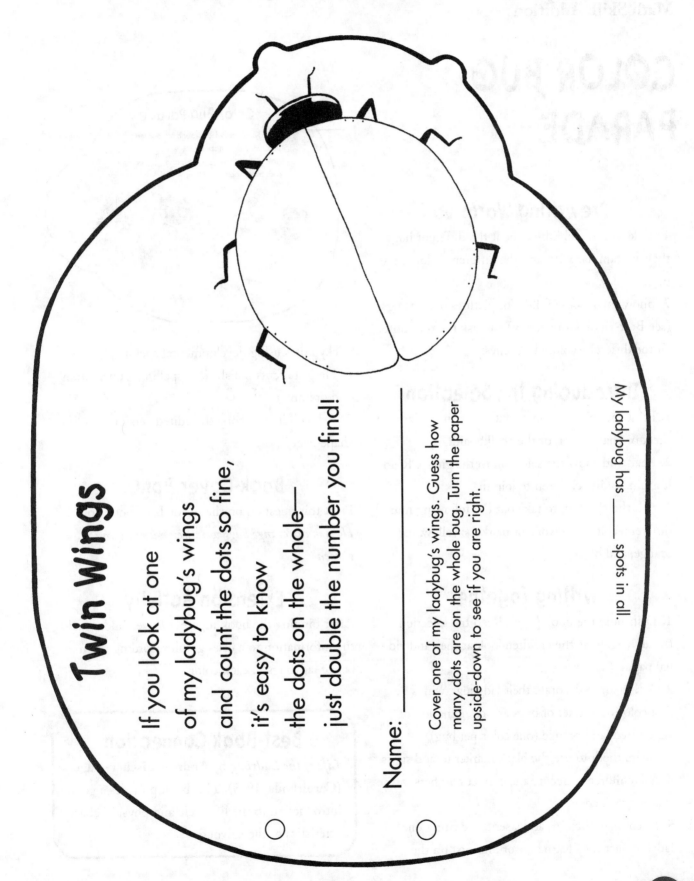

Twin Wings

If you look at one
of my ladybug's wings
and count the dots so fine,

it's easy to know
the dots on the whole—
just double the number you find!

Name: _____

Cover one of my ladybug's wings. Guess how many dots are on the whole bug. Turn the paper upside-down to see if you are right.

My ladybug has _____ spots in all.

COLOR BUG PARADE

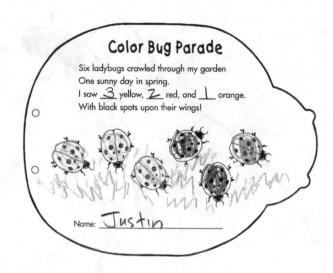

Color Bug Parade

Six ladybugs crawled through my garden
One sunny day in spring.
I saw _3_ yellow, _2_ red, and _1_ orange.
With black spots upon their wings!

Name: _Justin_

Prewriting Warm-up

1. Talk with the children about the different bugs they are familiar with and the different colors these bugs display.

2. Show them some full-color pictures of ladybugs (see Best-Book Connection) and ask them to note all the different-colored varieties.

Introducing the Selection

1. Print the selection onto sentence strips, a large sheet of chart paper, or the chalkboard.

2. Read and show the selection to the group. Read it again, asking children to join in.

3. Ask the children to take out the following four different-colored crayons or markers: yellow, red, orange, and black.

Writing Together

1. Distribute the book pages. Read the selection through again as the children look at their individual pages.

2. Ask them to decorate their ladybugs' wings by first coloring the set of bugs any combination of yellow, red, and orange (one color per bug).

3. Invite them to use the black marker to add spots.

4. Ask children to record the correct numbers in the spaces provided.

5. Encourage them to add a sentence citing one ladybug fact they learned, working first on the

sticky notes using developmental spelling.

6. Help students polish their spelling, punctuation, and grammar.

7. Ask children to copy the edited version onto the shape page.

Back-Cover Bonus

Print this question on the inside back book cover: *How many orange bugs were seen crawling in the garden?*

Extension Activity

After binding the book together, have children add the information to a class graph recording the number of ladybugs in each color.

Best-Book Connection

Life of the Ladybug by **Andreas Fischer-Nagel (Carolrhoda, 1985).** This book provides a good introduction to the life cycle and physical characteristics of the ladybug.

Little Ladybug Selection B Template

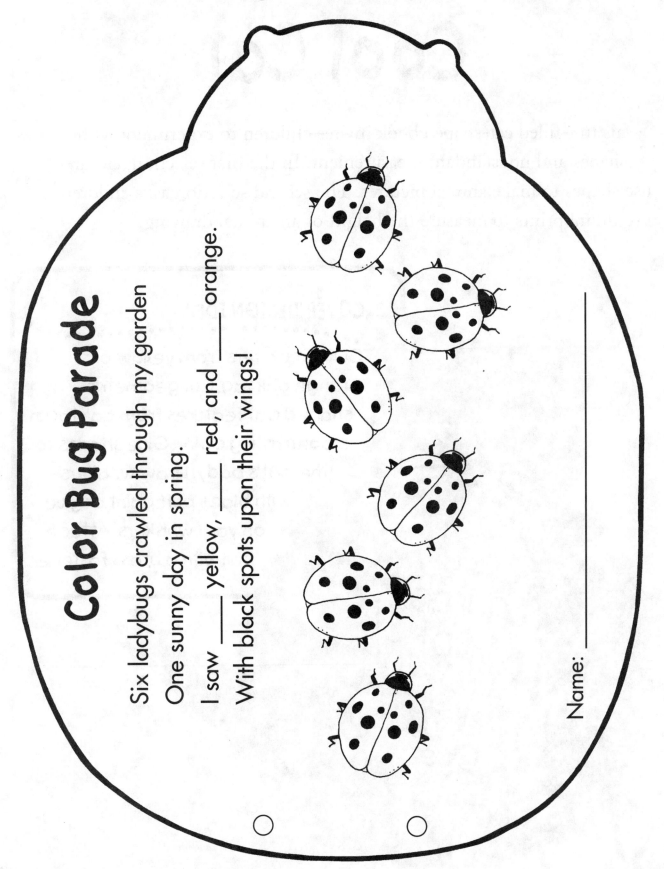

Color Bug Parade

Six ladybugs crawled through my garden
One sunny day in spring.
I saw ____ yellow, ____ red, and ____ orange.
With black spots upon their wings!

Name: _____

Cool Cat

This fun-filled cat-shaped book invites children to experiment with shapes and nonstandard measurement. In the first selection, children use shapes to make animal pictures. The second selection asks children to use thumbprints to measure the height of an animal drawing.

COVER DESIGN IDEA

Cut cat covers from yellow or orange oak tag. Cut geometric-shaped cat features from oak tag in a contrasting color. Glue shapes to the cat's body. Draw whiskers with black puff paint or glue on yarn whiskers. Attach tail with a brass fastener.

Thumbs Up!

by Mr. Lucero's Class

Cool Cat Cover Template

ANIMAL SHAPE SURPRISE

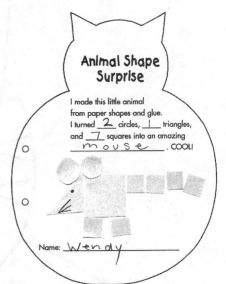

Animal Shape Surprise

I made this little animal from paper shapes and glue. I turned **2** circles, **1** triangles, and **7** squares into an amazing **mouse** . COOL!

Name: **Wendy**

Prewriting Warm-up

1. Show children some pre-cut paper shapes (circles, squares, and triangles).

2. Share the shape-inspired picture book *Picture Pie* by Ed Emberley (Little Brown, 1984). This book features pictures made from circles and circle pieces, but you can expand this concept by presenting an assortment of geometric shapes (circles, squares, and triangles) precut from construction paper.

3. Challenge each child to select shapes to arrange into animal pictures.

Introducing the Selection

1. Print the selection onto sentence strips, a large sheet of chart paper, or the chalkboard.

2. Read and show the selection to the group. Read it again, asking children to join in.

3. Tell children they are going to be making a book filled with animal pictures made from paper shapes.

Writing Together

1. Distribute the book pages, sticky notes for rough drafts, and the assortment of precut paper shapes. Read the selection through again as the children look at their individual pages.

2. Look together at the picture of the book cover. Ask children to take turns pointing out the geometric shapes that make up the cat. Ask them to arrange the precut shapes to create other animal pictures.

3. Meet individually with students and help them write descriptive labels for their pictures.

4. Invite children to use developmental spelling to record their ideas on sticky notes.

5. Help students polish their spelling, punctuation, and grammar.

6. Ask children to copy the edited version onto the shape page.

7. Invite children to use markers or crayons to add details to their pictures.

Back-Cover Bonus

Print this question on the inside back book cover: *Which animal is made of the most circles? The most triangles? The most squares?*

Extension Activity

After sharing the collaborative book, try making a cooperative class mural of paper shapes. Pick an animal theme—perhaps Underwater Animals or Rain Forest Animals. Cover a bulletin board with light-colored craft paper. Ask children to plan out the display and to divide up the tasks necessary to complete it. Finish the mural, using glue to attach shapes.

Best-Book Connection

Ed Emberley's *Picture Pie* (Little Brown, 1984). This book presents a multitude of pictures created from paper circles and pie-shaped circle pieces.

Cool Cat Selection A Template

Animal Shape Surprise

I made this little animal
from paper shapes and glue.
I turned _____ circles, _____ triangles,
and _____ squares into an amazing
_____ . COOL!

Name: _____

THUMBS UP!

Thumbs Up!

Animals grow to different sizes. Some are big and some are small. Look, I drew an animal and it's ___6___ thumbprints tall!

Name: Max

Prewriting Warm-up

1. One at a time, show children two pictures of animals almost the same height. Ask them to guess which is taller. How could they find out for sure?
2. Talk about measuring objects. Show children how to measure the animals by pressing a thumb in a washable ink pad and making a stack of thumbprints one on top of the other.
3. Tell the class they are going to draw their own animals and measure them

Introducing the Selection

1. Print the selection onto sentence strips, a large sheet of chart paper, or the chalkboard.
2. Read and show the selection to the group. Read it again, asking children to join in.
3. Tell the children they will be completing the selection by drawing a favorite animal and then using thumbprints to measure it.

Writing Together

1. Distribute the book pages and sticky notes for rough drafts. Read the selection through again as the children look at their individual pages.
2. Ask children to each choose one favorite animal to draw on their book page. (Use the title recommended in Best-Book Connection for inspiration.)
3. Invite children to press their thumbs into washable ink pads and then make thumbprints to measure the height of their animal drawings.
4. Invite them to write the name of their animals using developmental spelling and to record the number of thumbprints on the sticky notes.
5. Help students polish spelling, punctuation, and grammar.
6. Ask children to copy the edited version onto the shape page.

Back-Cover Bonus

Print these questions on the inside back book cover:
Which is the tallest animal drawing in the book?
Which is the shortest?

Extension Activity

Have children make thumbprint rulers by printing thumbprints on pieces of oak tag cut to approximately the size of a bookmark. Help each child number their thumbprints (which should just touch at the edges). Prepare a measurement hunt in which children use the rulers to find things you describe according to their measurements. Can they, for example, find something that is 3 thumbprints long or 6 thumbprints wide?

Best-Book Connection

Ed Emberley's *Drawing Book: Make a World* (Little Brown, 1972). A great resource for inspiring children's animal drawings.

Cool Cat Selection B Template

Thumbs Up!

Animals grow to different sizes.
Some are big and some are small.
Look, I drew an animal
and it's _____ thumbprints tall!

Name: _____

Pizza to Go!

What a yummy way to learn math! These pizza-shaped selections will give children a taste of fractions and a chance to count and record their favorite toppings. So, dig in!

COVER DESIGN IDEA

Cut covers from tan-colored oak tag. Color edges with brown marker to make the crust. Scribble pizza with red marker to simulate tomato sauce. Glue on white yarn "cheese" and brown felt circles to represent pepperoni and/or mushrooms.

Pizza to Go! Cover Template

CAN YOU TOP THIS?

Prewriting Warm-up

1. Ask children to talk about pizza preferences. If they like pizza, do they prefer homemade pizza or would they rather order it from a pizzeria? What kinds of toppings, if any, do they enjoy?

2. Tell the class they are going to make a pizza-shaped book that will give them a chance to tell what pizza toppings they like.

Introducing the Selection

1. Print the selection onto sentence strips, a large sheet of chart paper, or the chalkboard.

2. Read and show the selection to the group. Read it again, asking children to join in.

3. Tell children they will complete the selection by checking off and then adding up the number of pizza toppings they like.

Writing Together

1. Distribute the book pages and sticky notes for rough drafts. Read the selection through again as the children look at their individual pages.

2. Ask them to check off as many toppings as they like and to use the sticky notes to write the names of any other toppings they would like to add.

3. Help students polish their spelling, punctuation, and grammar.

4. Ask children to copy the edited toppings onto the blank spaces on in the poem.

5. Invite them to add an illustration to the page.

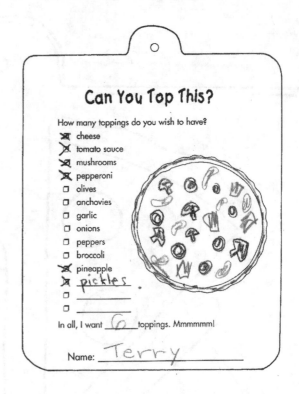

Can You Top This?

How many toppings do you wish to have?

- ☒ cheese
- ☒ tomato sauce
- ☒ mushrooms
- ☒ pepperoni
- ☐ olives
- ☐ anchovies
- ☐ garlic
- ☐ onions
- ☐ peppers
- ☐ broccoli
- ☒ pineapple
- ☒ pickles
- ☐ _____
- ☐ _____

In all, I want ___6___ toppings. Mmmmmm!

Name: __Terry__

Back-Cover Bonus

Print this question on the inside back book cover: *Which topping was the class favorite?*

Extension Activity

After sharing the collaborative book, talk about the toppings everyone likes and dislikes. Then plan a homemade pizza-pie party. Provide prepared pizza-pie shells (available in grocery stores). Have children contribute sauce and toppings from home and let them add these to the pizza. Bake and enjoy!

Best-Book Connection

Hold the Anchovies! A Book About Pizza by **Shelly Rotner (Orchard Books, 1996).** A photo-essay about pizza from start to finish.

Pizza to Go! Selection A Template

Can You Top This?

How many toppings do you wish to have?

- ☐ cheese
- ☐ tomato sauce
- ☐ mushrooms
- ☐ pepperoni
- ☐ olives
- ☐ anchovies
- ☐ garlic
- ☐ onions
- ☐ peppers
- ☐ broccoli
- ☐ pineapple
- ☐ _____
- ☐ _____
- ☐ _____

In all, I want _____ toppings. Mmmmmm!

Name: _____

PIZZA PIECES

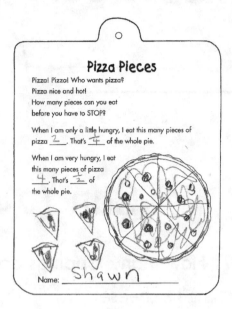

Prewriting Warm-up

1. Ask children to tell of occasions when their family enjoys pizza such as birthday parties or Friday nights.

2. Ask children to tell how many pieces of pizza they usually eat at a time. How many pieces do the older children and grown-ups they know eat?

Introducing the Selection

1. Print the selection onto sentence strips, a large sheet of chart paper, or the chalkboard.

2. Read and show the selection to the group. Read it again, asking children to join in.

3. Tell the children they are going to be making a book that will give them a chance to tell about how much pizza they eat.

Writing Together

1. Distribute the book pages and sticky notes for rough drafts. Read the selection through again as the children look at their individual pages.

2. Ask children to think about how much pizza they eat when they are only a little bit hungry and when they are very hungry. Help them translate the number of pieces they eat (as recorded in the first and third blank spaces) into fractional equivalents (to be recorded in the second and fourth blank spaces). **Tip:** Have children look at the book cover to determine how many pieces they might eat from an average-size pie.

3. Invite them to use developmental spelling to write their ideas on the sticky notes.

4. Help students polish their spelling, punctuation, and grammar.

5. Ask children to copy the edited version onto their shape page. Invite them to add an illustration and label it, if they wish.

Back-Cover Bonus

Print this question on the inside back cover:
How many children like to eat two pieces of pizza when they are hungry?

Extension Activity

Bring in an assortment of the foods portrayed in the book *Eating Fractions* and have children use plastic knives and cutting boards to cut the foods into fractional pieces. Children can then sample the treats and note the fractional amounts they ate.

Best-Book Connection

Eating Fractions **by Bruce McMillan (Scholastic, 1991).** Vivid photographs of food—including pizza—are shown cut into various fractional pieces, teaching the concepts of halves, thirds, and fourths.

Pizza Pieces

Pizza! Pizza! Who wants pizza?

Pizza nice and hot!

How many pieces can you eat

before you have to STOP?

When I am only a little hungry, I eat this many pieces of

pizza: _____. That's _____ of the whole pie.

When I am very hungry, I eat
this many pieces of pizza:
_____. That's _____ of
the whole pie.

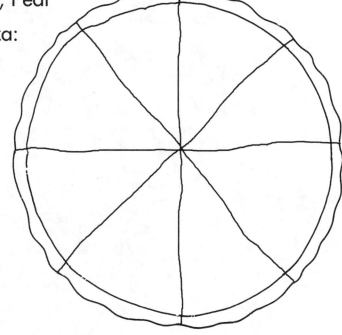

Name: _____